NOVELS BY DON DELILLO

Americana

End Zone

Great Jones Street

Ratner's Star

Players

Running Dog

The Names

White Noise

THE DAY ROOM

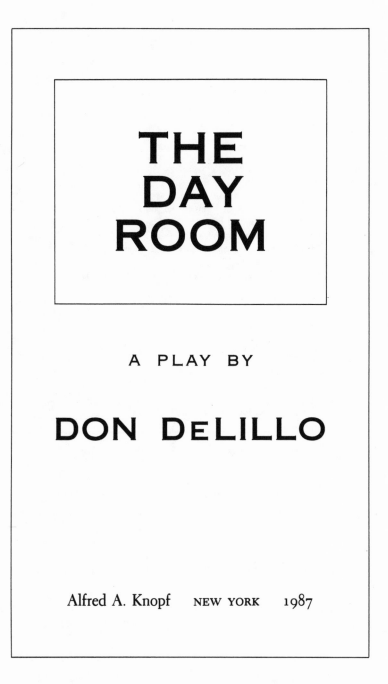

THE DAY ROOM

A PLAY BY

DON DeLILLO

Alfred A. Knopf   NEW YORK   1987

THIS IS A BORZOI BOOK
PUBLISHED BY ALFRED A. KNOPF, INC.

Originally published in *American Theatre*, September 1986.

Library of Congress Cataloging-in-Publication Data

DeLillo, Don.
  The day room.

  I. Title.
PS3554.E4425D39   1987   812'.54   87-46039
ISBN 0-394-56918-0

Manufactured in the United States of America

FIRST EDITION

The Day Room was first presented by the American Repertory Theater in April 1986, in Cambridge, Massachusetts, under the direction of Michael Bloom.

In October 1986 the A.R.T. company performed the play in Los Angeles, San Diego, and Palo Alto. The play was restaged in Cambridge in the spring of 1987, with David Wheeler directing.

The play opened in New York in December 1987 at the Manhattan Theater Club under the direction of Michael Blakemore.

The Day Room was originally developed in a workshop at the Sundance Institute.

THE DAY ROOM

ACT ONE

Budge, a man in his sixties

Wyatt, a younger man

Grass, a man of indeterminate age

Nurse Walker, a white woman

Dr. Phelps, a young man

Nurse Baker, a black woman

Dr. Bazelon, a man in his forties

Male orderly

Female orderly

Morning.

A hospital room. Two beds, two night tables with telephones, two wardrobe units, several chairs. Doors to the hallway and the bathroom.

Dim light. A single figure.

It is Budge, engaged in his daily round of tai chi, the ancient Chinese discipline of exercise and meditation. He wears slippers and white pajamas. His motions are slow, stylized, continuous, with a weightless quality. He does movements called "Draw the Bow" and "Wave Hands Like Clouds."

Lights slowly up.

Wyatt occupies the bed by the bathroom door. He is sitting up, reading the Wall Street Journal.

When Budge is finished with his exercises, he goes to the other bed, climbs in, sits erect.

Wyatt stops reading. There is a self-conscious moment.

                BUDGE
In other words you're not a talker.

                WYATT
I don't have the knack. It's a gift. Some people have it.

BUDGE

But aren't we here, in a sense, to talk? Isn't that the point?
We're even dressed for conversation. Look. Loose-fitting
clothes, so we can gesture freely, relax, unwind, unburden
ourselves.

WYATT

I'm here for tests.

BUDGE

But in the meantime. Two people alone, a common history
and anatomy, suitably dressed, in a semiprivate room. Mr.
Wyatt, what better opportunity? We have all the essentials.
Beds, chairs, regulated temperature. We don't have to go
home to sleep, then come back here to talk. The beds are
here and so are we. They bring in food. The food is on the
premises. We don't have to interrupt our talk to go outside
and hunt around for a decent restaurant, quiet, affordable,
with unobtrusive waiters, subdued lighting, tables not too
close together, where we can enjoy the free play of a mutual
exchange, over a hearty and nourishing meal, without
clashing utensils, on a sidestreet, with trees. It's all right
here. Everything is arranged.

WYATT

They shouldn't call it semiprivate.

BUDGE

In other words it's either private or not private. How can
something be semiprivate?

WYATT

Exactly.

BUDGE

A canny insight. See? I never thought of that. Things come
out in casual talk. It's the setting. The setting is favorable.
It's all but perfect.

6

WYATT

Words come hard for me, Mr. Budge.

BUDGE

See? In hospitals, people are polite. They call each other mister, doctor. There's a little element of formality. It's conducive to good talk. There's a dignity, a tradition. We don't have that out there.

WYATT

Except on airplanes.

BUDGE

People are polite on airplanes. You may be right.

WYATT

Great humpbacked jets, screaming through the sky.

BUDGE

There's a whole thrilling layer of politeness, especially in the last few seconds before takeoff, on a transoceanic flight, at sunset, with a crew of sixteen, twenty-four.

WYATT

Multiples of eight.

BUDGE

Going down the runway, everyone belted in, assigned letters and numbers. The landscape hurtling past, the temperature regulated—

WYATT

We sense the presence of death.

BUDGE

Of what?

WYATT

The hush of death. On airplanes, in hospitals.

BUDGE

And this makes people a little polite, a little deferential. See?
We're moving right along. Talk is a passion with me. It has
to be good talk, of course. Good talk is the keynote. I
admire the European experience. Cafés, cigarette smoke.
Talk becomes more passionate as you travel east. Paris,
Rome, Athens. An intensity enters the voice. Words take on
deeper meaning. There is a life-force in the simplest
greeting. An urge toward well-being, intimacy, survival. The
whole point is to keep each other company. Other people's
voices keep us company, make survival possible under the
cruelest conditions. Look at the Arab experience. People
dress for conversation. Flowing garments, sandals, dark
beards. What kind of tests are they doing?

WYATT

Standard series. It's something I like to do every few years.
Check myself into a hospital. Get a good rest.

BUDGE

I thought that was something movie stars did. Notorious
alcoholics.

WYATT

My coverage provides.

BUDGE

If the coverage is there, you'd be foolish not to.

WYATT

The total system needs to slow down, without the usual
distractions.

BUDGE

Haile Selassie used to see his doctor every two hours.

WYATT

They'll look at my cardiovascular, my respiratory.

BUDGE

He was the Lion of Judah.

WYATT

They'll reassure me. That's basically what this is all about.
Rest. Reassurance.

> *Grass enters, in an open robe and drooping pajamas,*
> *dragging with him a metal stand with a crosspiece on*
> *which are arrayed a number of bottles and pouches*
> *containing fluids of various colors. Intravenous tubes*
> *run from the bottles to different parts of Grass's body,*
> *entering the pajamas under the sleeves, through the fly,*
> *etc. He is unshaved, wears old running shoes, moves*
> *into the room at an exceedingly slow pace.*

GRASS

My building's going co-op.

BUDGE

This is Mr. Grass. He likes to pay visits. Maybe because
nobody comes to see him.

GRASS

I'm an acquired taste.

WYATT

Isn't he awfully sick to be walking around like this?

GRASS

I have my dangling paraphernalia. It feeds me, it washes me,
it restarts my heart, it purifies my fluids. It *is* my fluids in
some cases.

BUDGE

In other words some of it is yours, pumped out of your body,
only to return in purified form.

9

GRASS

Some of it is mine, some of it is mass-produced in the
Republic of Korea. It's polyester blood. Pick your own color.

WYATT

What is your trouble, Mr. Grass?

GRASS

I've got heavy water.

BUDGE

Heavy water?

WYATT

Isn't that what they use in nuclear reactors?

BUDGE

I know I've heard the term.

WYATT

It's one of those terms you run across when you read about
near disasters. There's a whole battery of terms. Heavy water.

BUDGE

Alkaline rain.

WYATT

Sulfate emissions.

BUDGE

Thermal inversions.

WYATT

Benzene intoxications.

BUDGE

We're moving right along. I'm pleased to see how well we're progressing.

GRASS (*to Wyatt*)

And you are Mr.—

WYATT

Wyatt.

GRASS

A promising idea for a name.

WYATT

It's not an idea for a name. It is a name.

GRASS

Could be improved with a little work.

WYATT

I'm Wyatt. I like being Wyatt.

GRASS

Who else have you tried?

WYATT

I didn't know there was a choice.

GRASS

There's always a choice. Do I buy my apartment or keep renting?

BUDGE

His wife is on the tenants' committee.

GRASS
It fills the space in her life that used to be occupied by sex
and violence.

BUDGE
He says she never visits.

GRASS
She has her bridge club. She has tennis in a bubble. There's
antiquing on the weekend in the country. Her bow and arrow.
Her insect larvae. There's her foot fetish. Her bicycling
through the wine country. She has her massive coronaries.

BUDGE
Mr. Grass believes in equity.

GRASS
I live in a great steel tower that reflects the blazing sun.
People catch fire just walking by. The more bodies that pile
up around you, the greater your equity, the stronger your
power, the longer you live. This is the point of living in a
high rise. To see the bodies pile up at sunset, the nostalgic
hour, the hour of summing up, stirring the cocktails, feeling
the great tower sway in the hot winds. Where do you live,
Mr. Wyatt?

WYATT
In a frame house, with a small yard, on a quiet street.

GRASS
You're as good as dead.

BUDGE
I like Mr. Grass, regardless. There's something about him—

WYATT
A kind of runaway quality.

BUDGE

—that fosters conversation.

GRASS (*to Wyatt*)

What color is your blood?

WYATT

Red.

GRASS

Red. Me too. Acrylic or polyester?

WYATT

It's mine, it's human.

GRASS

I've invested heavily in blood futures. I have a direct line to
the trading floor for polyester blood. There's a heaving mass
of men crying out their bids. The blood arrives at the
warehouse in the form of double-knit suits. It's the only kind
of suit I wear. When I collapse in the street, paramedics
rush me to the hospital, liquefy the suit and inject it in my
veins.

WYATT

Then what?

GRASS

The nurse walks in the door.

Nurse Walker enters.

NURSE WALKER

All right, Mr. Grass. It's time you were heading back.

*She begins to disconnect him from the apparatus of
bottles and tubes.*

13

Dr. Phelps enters.

WYATT
What's going on?

GRASS
What's going on?

DR. PHELPS (*to Wyatt*)
You're new on the floor, aren't you? I'm Dr. Phelps. What can I say except terribly, terribly sorry? I wish I could tell you it hasn't happened before. It has.

WYATT
Who is he?

GRASS
Who is he?

NURSE WALKER
Three times to be exact.

DR. PHELPS
He's completely harmless. What happens is, he slips out of the Arno Klein Psychiatric Wing, sneaks through the common lobby, gets on an elevator, finds an IV setup, attaches himself, and then just walks around, visiting.

NURSE WALKER
He wants a little attention, that's all.

DR. PHELPS
He's perfectly harmless.

BUDGE
He wants a little company, a little palaver.

14

WYATT
And he doesn't need that contraption?

DR. PHELPS
He's a healthy man, physically, despite appearances. You're
Dr. Bazelon's patient. Routine tests, am I right?

WYATT
Strictly standard.

DR. PHELPS
Good.

WYATT
The most basic tests there are.

DR. PHELPS
Very good.

WYATT
Completely and totally nonthreatening.

DR. PHELPS
Fine.

GRASS
There's a huge body of work, yet to be written, on the
subject of brightness. "Brightness falls from the air." This is
the only thing they've written so far, of all the things that
could be written, on a subject so vast and dazzling.

DR. PHELPS
I'll just escort our friend back out to the nurses' station. Be
assured: it won't happen again.

WYATT
Thank you.

BUDGE
Thank you, doctor.

Dr. Phelps exits with Grass and the intravenous setup.

NURSE WALKER
Whenever I think my job is tough, I think of the nurses in
the other wing.

BUDGE
What do you mean?

NURSE WALKER
They get droolers and hysterics. They get psychotic episodes,
we only get traumas. They get fantasies, we get death.

WYATT
What's easy about death?

NURSE WALKER
It's so predictable. Lately it seems I'm spending all my time
washing dead bodies before we send them to the morgue.

BUDGE
I didn't know you had to do that.

NURSE WALKER
The nurse who takes care of a patient when he's sick and in
pain is the nurse who washes the corpse. This is the custom
and I think it's a good one. I feel reverent, standing behind
the bed curtain, at dusk, in winter, washing the corpse,
wrapping it up in a morgue sheet, wrapping a bed sheet
around the morgue sheet. I feel I'm doing something ancient
and sacred. They usually die at dusk, in winter. There's
something about a wintry dusk. I feel it myself. Something
lonely in the bone.

BUDGE

Then what?

NURSE WALKER

There's a procedure for getting the corpse down to the morgue. It is doubly or triply wrapped. It is wheeled on a morgue cart with a stretcher tied down over the wrapping. It looks like something else completely. Some shapeless, harmless, innocent hospital object. So patients won't be frightened and depressed. Imagine getting on an elevator. And there's a body on a cart. And the attendant presses M—for morgue, mortuary, muffled drums. And down you all go.

Dr. Phelps enters.

DR. PHELPS

What did I miss?

WYATT

I was wondering about breakfast.

DR. PHELPS

I hope Mr. Grass didn't upset you. We could restrain him but that would be extreme.

WYATT

Restrain him how?

DR. PHELPS

A jacket restraint.

BUDGE

You mean one of those long-sleeved things from the movies where orderlies come running down the hall and bind the person's arms to his body and cinch the ends tight. Actors love doing mad scenes.

17

DR. PHELPS
It's so close to their experience.

WYATT
In other words a straitjacket.

DR. PHELPS
They don't call it that anymore.

NURSE WALKER
That word became too blunt, too crude.

DR. PHELPS
Too restrictive. So they called it a camisole.

NURSE WALKER
Women were going mad in greater numbers.

DR. PHELPS
They wanted a softer term.

NURSE WALKER
Feminine.

DR. PHELPS
Airy.

NURSE WALKER
Seductive.

DR. PHELPS
When camisole ran its course, they decided to call it a
posey.

NURSE WALKER
Because it rhymes with cozy.

DR. PHELPS (*to Wyatt*)
We speak of a patient being poseyed into a wheelchair, poseyed into a bed or onto a toilet.

NURSE WALKER
Just so you know the jargon.

DR. PHELPS
Now that you're here. I'll show you how we slip one on. Extend your arms.

WYATT
I don't like being the center of attention.

DR. PHELPS
But this is what hospitals are for. So a person can follow his disease into the ultraviolet light.

NURSE WALKER
Disease itself is not unhealthy. We recover from disease.

DR. PHELPS
Disease is not the illness. Disease is just a symptom of the illness.

WYATT
What is the illness?

NURSE WALKER
Knowing that you're going to die.

WYATT (*to Budge*)
Why are they saying these things?

DR. PHELPS
Because we have to say something. Because language itself

would be enormously impoverished if we didn't have disease to talk about.

NURSE WALKER
Haven't you ever heard a patient flaunt the terminology of his disease?

DR. PHELPS
They become experts overnight.

NURSE WALKER
They feel at home in the language of their disease.

DR. PHELPS
It's their disease after all.

NURSE WALKER
They love to explain the terms to visitors.

DR. PHELPS
We have to name these conditions as they appear and proliferate. We have to design a body of words as vivid and horrifying as the conditions they attempt to describe.

NURSE WALKER
If the gravity of the disease is not reflected in the terminology, the patient feels cheated.

DR. PHELPS
We have to stretch the language to its breaking point as people find new ways to die, abrupt and mysterious symptomatologies.

NURSE WALKER
Sarcomas.

DR. PHELPS
Blastomas.

NURSE WALKER
I love the gleam of hospital corridors in the dead of night.

DR. PHELPS *(to Wyatt)*
There is only one center of attention. You ring a bell,
someone comes. You cry out in pain, we try to comfort you.

NURSE WALKER
We wash your body when you die.

BUDGE
I have to admit I never thought about what happens after I
take my last breath.

DR. PHELPS
Who would wash your body if you'd stayed at home?

BUDGE
I never thought about the inconvenience I'd be causing.

NURSE WALKER
What I wonder about is the narrow scope of the roles we
have to play. Can't we stop being doctor and nurse for just a
minute? Can't we give you a glimpse of the people behind
the uniforms? People with their own doubts, fears—

DR. PHELPS
Sicknesses.

NURSE WALKER
We get sick.

DR. PHELPS
We cry out.

NURSE WALKER
People with their own secrets, their intimate systems of
protection.

DR. PHELPS
What lies beneath?

NURSE WALKER
One level.

DR. PHELPS
Two levels.

NURSE WALKER
Wait right here.

DR. PHELPS
Keep waiting.

NURSE WALKER
One sunny day.

DR. PHELPS
You'll wake up.

NURSE WALKER
And this will all be gone.

DR. PHELPS
Disappeared.

NURSE WALKER
Mysteriously.

BUDGE
The interplay is delightful.

DR. PHELPS
Replaced by something totally—

NURSE WALKER
—strange.

22

DR. PHELPS
And white.

NURSE WALKER
And dangerous.

WYATT
Mr. Budge, do these people belong here?

DR. PHELPS
He wants to know if we're from Arno Klein. But he's embarrassed to ask.

NURSE WALKER
I find that attractive in a man.

BUDGE
I don't know anything you don't know. I've seen Mr. Grass before. But not these two.

WYATT
How long have you been here?

BUDGE
I'm a readmission. Four days, this trip.

WYATT
Have you heard of a Dr. Phelps?

BUDGE
No.

WYATT
Did they get rid of Mr. Grass just to take his place? Is that the idea?

DR. PHELPS
Is that the idea?

BUDGE

They seem harmless enough.

WYATT

I don't think they're harmless.

BUDGE

They seem intelligent—literate.

WYATT

That makes it all the worse. All the crazier. Don't you see?

NURSE WALKER

Don't you see?

Nurse Baker enters.

NURSE BAKER

So here they are.

WYATT

Here they are.

NURSE BAKER

On my floor.

WYATT

In our room.

NURSE BAKER

I thought they'd try any floor but mine.

Wyatt waves his copy of the newspaper.

WYATT

The news is full of hospital accidents. Fatal injections.
"WOMAN EXPLODES ON OPERATING TABLE." How can they be

24

allowed to run loose like this? Doesn't anyone keep track of
the inmates over there?

> NURSE BAKER

That's a strong word.

> WYATT

That's a polite word.

> NURSE BAKER

They're not perpetrators of violent crimes.

> WYATT

They're crazy people. They're confined. Theoretically.

> NURSE BAKER

An inmate, when I hear that word, that's a criminal type.
That's bull-necked, sleepy-eyed, squat. A person with serious
tattoos.

> WYATT

But what are they doing here?

> BUDGE

Are they taunting us? Is it a form of ridicule?

> NURSE BAKER

Just so we all know, these are people who spend their days in
a place called the day room. Painted pure white, coat after
coat after coat. Lonely monologues bouncing off the walls.
People dragging through, day after day after day, with a kind
of scuffling noise like half-drunk commuters trying to catch
their trains. They watch daytime TV and throw food. They're
on a soft-food regimen to keep them from injuring each other.

> BUDGE

They don't look or sound like people who throw food.

NURSE BAKER

There's a soft-food ward. There's a ward where they watch daytime TV even at night.

Dr. Phelps and Nurse Walker listen attentively.

BUDGE

How do you know all this?

NURSE BAKER

I snuck over once, just to see.

WYATT

See what?

NURSE BAKER

What it's like, in disguise, not wearing my uniform, so I could mingle unannounced. The whole room's fluorescent. You hear the sizzling lights. And they sit there faceless, in soft white chairs, with crayons and paper.

BUDGE

Aren't crayons dangerous?

NURSE BAKER

Everything's dangerous. In the day room, a speck of dust is charged with danger. A little mote dancing in the air gives off danger signals, weird static. People say things out of nowhere. The smallest word is packed with danger. It's all a danger. It's all white. The walls, the lights, the food, the crayons, the paper.

WYATT

What's the point of giving out white crayons and white paper? They can't see what they draw.

NURSE BAKER

They don't draw. They dress up. Just like you see. They steal

uniforms from the laundry and pretend they're us. Sometimes
they don't even sneak out. They stay in the day room,
dressed up like all *kinds* of people. But these two, you can
put your minds at rest. They are totally out of options.
Believe me. They won't be back.

She exits with Dr. Phelps and Nurse Walker.

WYATT
It's incredible. It's an outrage.

BUDGE
We're hospital patients. Vulnerable.

WYATT
Susceptible to every kind of abuse.

BUDGE
We're dependent on these people.

WYATT
Like an airliner roaring off a runway—

BUDGE
—into a steep climb.

WYATT
We depend on the crew. It's the same thing exactly. And
we still haven't been fed. No one's fed us.

BUDGE
Ring the call bell.

WYATT
You ring the call bell.

BUDGE
I don't mind missing a meal now and then.

WYATT

I'm lodging a massive complaint.

BUDGE

At least they got you to talking, those two. For once I
didn't have to initiate things. I remember outside Cairo
once, my late wife and I found a café with a dirt floor.
We'd been looking for this café for weeks. It was one of the
last of the dirt-floor cafés. Wonderful conversations, ideal
conditions. The chairs don't scrape as they do on wood
floors or tile floors, interrupting the talk, when people get
up. Plates and glasses break soundlessly, falling to the dirt,
when waiters drop them. The talk swirls and eddies. The
smoke collects in the air. Tourists undergo terrible hardships
just to find this place. My wife and I used to sit there,
watching them straggle in. They were delighted by the
floor. All the rumors confirmed, all the efforts redeemed.
"Dirt floors! Dirt!" My God they were happy, and so were
we. But in the end it was the talk that really gripped us. We
came for the dirt but stayed for the talk. To watch an
Egyptian talk, or a Tunisian in a leisure suit. What intimacy
in the sound of those voices, in the faces and gestures. Such
intense and open need. The talk eddies and swirls. The
broken glass gleams in the dirt. More tourists all the time,
arriving on air-conditioned buses, crowding in to watch the
Kuwaitis talk, the Omanis who've come all this way just
to talk, the Yemenis in from the Empty Quarter, the
Saudis in immaculate white robes, wearing hammered-gold
watches, engaged in undisguised talk. How I miss the
East.

WYATT

I like to travel. But somehow we never seem—

BUDGE

Tell me about yourself.

WYATT

There's nothing to tell. I just want to get these tests
completed so I can go home to my wife and children.

BUDGE

Wife and children. What a picture that conjures up. The
interplay must be astonishing. My wife wasn't able. We kept
on hoping she'd present me with a child. What a wonderful
verbal concept. To be presented with a child. We thought
of adopting, of course. I saw myself as head of a brood. One
of those teeming multinational families from the Sunday
supplements. Eight, nine, ten kids from the Mideast, the Far
East, the Horn of Africa. Someone to talk to, passionately,
in my old age.

Dr. Bazelon enters.

WYATT

Dr. Bazelon, what a relief. Do you know what's been going
on here?

DR. BAZELON

I stopped at the nurses' station. They're pretty shamefaced
out there. Two episodes, was it?

WYATT

Two episodes, three people.

DR. BAZELON

Inexcusable. Security is built into the system. But the system
sometimes fails. (*To Budge*) I'm Dr. Bazelon.

BUDGE

Are you a private corporation?

WYATT

They're all private corporations.

BUDGE

I would never go to a doctor who wasn't.

WYATT

They have to be, for their own self-respect.

DR. BAZELON

Are you about ready, Larry?

WYATT

Ready for what?

DR. BAZELON

They'll be taking you down in ten minutes.

WYATT

I thought the tests were scheduled for early morning.

DR. BAZELON

We never do these tests in the morning.

WYATT

I thought I understood tomorrow morning. I'm not sure I'm prepared.

DR. BAZELON

You haven't eaten, have you?

WYATT

They didn't bring the food.

DR. BAZELON

They weren't supposed to bring the food. You're not supposed to eat before these tests. When you come back up, you can eat.

WYATT
Shouldn't they bring food for Mr. Budge?

BUDGE
They probably have it on my Kardex: Light eater. When
they have time, maybe a little something. No hurry, no
bother. Whenever it's convenient.

DR. BAZELON
First, Larry, there are some things I want to go over with
you.

WYATT
All right.

DR. BAZELON
Are you sleeping?

WYATT
Pretty well. Adequately.

DR. BAZELON
Which is it?

WYATT
Most nights, pretty well.

DR. BAZELON
Wake up at any point?

WYATT
Sometimes.

DR. BAZELON
What, noises in the street, planes passing over? Or just
wake up, stare into the dark?

                    WYATT
Just wake up.

                    DR. BAZELON
Stare into the dark?

                    WYATT
Yes.

                    DR. BAZELON
Are you eating?

                    WYATT
Appetite's fine. I try to avoid red meat, fried foods,
processed foods—

                    DR. BAZELON
Are you breathing? Is it quiet breathing—rhythmic,
measured?

                    WYATT
Sometimes, on a steep flight of stairs, or running for a bus,
in the rain—

                    DR. BAZELON
You have to catch your breath.

                    WYATT
I have to stop.

                    DR. BAZELON
To catch your breath.

                    WYATT
Yes.

                    DR. BAZELON
But it's there. You do catch it.

WYATT

Yes.

DR. BAZELON

When you blink, do you experience difficulty re-opening your eyes?

WYATT

After they close, you mean.

DR. BAZELON

Do they open automatically?

WYATT

Or do I have to think about it.

DR. BAZELON

Are you working?

WYATT

Quite hard. Harder than usual.

DR. BAZELON

Which is it?

WYATT

Harder than usual.

DR. BAZELON

Are you walking?

WYATT

I try to walk whenever possible, for the exercise.

DR. BAZELON

Describe your stride.

WYATT

I take short strides.

DR. BAZELON
Are you sure? Think about it. Take your time.

WYATT
I take long strides.

DR. BAZELON
Good. Are they confident?

WYATT
Long, confident strides. Exactly.

DR. BAZELON
Are you talking? More than you were? Less than you were?

WYATT
About the same.

DR. BAZELON
Say something.

WYATT
Oh boy.

DR. BAZELON
I want to hear you talk.

WYATT
What can I say? The hardest thing about grade school was being called on to recite. I used to dread it. Slump way down in my seat.

DR. BAZELON
Say anything at all.

WYATT
Give me just a second.

34

DR. BAZELON
The range is wide, Larry.

WYATT
Anything at all.

DR. BAZELON
The world is spread before us.

WYATT
I get a little tense.

DR. BAZELON
Answer carefully now.

WYATT
It would help if I knew what other people say.

DR. BAZELON
Are your bowels regular? Are you crapping? Describe your
stool for me.

WYATT
Firm, solid, compact.

DR. BAZELON
Which is it?

WYATT
Firm.

DR. BAZELON
Tell me about the color of your stool.

WYATT
Brown.

DR. BAZELON

Dark, light? I shouldn't have to prompt.

WYATT

Mid-brown.

DR. BAZELON

Do you feel it's yours and no one else's? Do you feel
intimately connected to it?

WYATT

Yes.

DR. BAZELON

Would you know it if you came upon it unexpectedly, in a
meadow, say, or on a moor?

WYATT

Can we come back to that?

DR. BAZELON

When you put your weight on one foot, does it tend to be
your right foot or your left foot?

WYATT

My left.

DR. BAZELON

Take your time.

WYATT

My right.

DR. BAZELON

Good. It's almost time now. They'll be coming to take you
down. How is Angela by the way?

36

WYATT

She's fine, doctor.

DR. BAZELON

How are the girls?

WYATT

You mean the boys.

DR. BAZELON

Of course. You'll be back up in two hours. I'll see that lunch is brought right in.

BUDGE

You say these tests are never done in the morning. Why is that?

DR. BAZELON

It's the half-light. It causes a patient to feel a certain deep-reaching dread. A stranger walks into the room, wakes up the patient, says, "We're taking you down now." It's barely past dawn. The sad, pale hour. The patient feels defenseless, due to his half-waking state, the voice of the stranger in the room, the white walls down there, the gleaming instruments, the men and women wearing masks. But mostly it's the half-light, we find, that troubles him. So we schedule these tests for the period of maximum natural radiance. The room is sunlit, immersed in warm, wide, reassuring light. We make it a point to wheel the patient past the solarium, where fellow patients sit facing into the sun, amid hanging plants, talking and reading, some of them poseyed into wheelchairs for their own good.

WYATT

Why should I experience dread, at any hour? You told me these were routine tests. "Unremarkable" was the word you used. I'm here mainly to rest. The tests are a form of reassurance, like the sunlit room, the hanging plants.

DR. BAZELON

We want to use ultrasound. We want to bombard your tissues with high-frequency sound waves, strictly as a precaution, a pre-emptive strike, to halt the growth of questionable tissue.

WYATT

What kind of sound waves?

DR. BAZELON

Tapes of the cries of baby mice. This sound reaches a level of forty thousand cycles per second. It's the purest thing in nature.

WYATT

Was I aware of this, doctor? Did you tell me this?

DR. BAZELON

I first became acquainted with this technique when I was at medical school, offshore, in the Amazon Basin. I've used it successfully many, many times.

WYATT

Did I know you went to medical school outside the U.S.?

DR. BAZELON

I'm not ashamed of it. Fifty-five medical schools in this country turned me down. So what? They turn down thousands upon thousands every year. What is the third world for if not to provide a haven for people like me? I went to the Amazon, to the universidad, built on stilts, in the shoals and swamps. Bodies for our dissection class came straight from the jungle. First they were people, then they were corpses, finally cadavers. What a melancholy transition. Some of them fellow students, from places like Middletown and Bay City, clawed to death by jaguars with topaz eyes.

38

BUDGE

Are you sure this is Dr. Bazelon?

DR. BAZELON

The jungle is stunning at dawn.

WYATT

This is Bazelon. I know him. We play golf.

DR. BAZELON

Sometimes I'm amazed myself. The things they come up
with. Dazzling advances every day. Extraordinary to live in
such an age. Marvelous, marvelous moments. Extend your
arms, Larry, would you, for just a second?

WYATT

What for?

DR. BAZELON

Just hold your arms out, please, full length.

Nurse Baker enters.

*Dr. Bazelon slumps, becomes passive and
uncomprehending.*

NURSE BAKER

So here he is. Look at him. The dawn of man.

WYATT

But this is a doctor. A real doctor. It's Dr. Bazelon. I know
him.

NURSE BAKER

This is no Bazelon. This one? You must be kidding.

WYATT

But I know him. He's been my doctor for years. We play
golf, racquetball. We're friends.

39

NURSE BAKER

You want me to believe you reveal your body to this man on a regular basis?

WYATT

We go to the theater. He and I. His wife and my wife. It's got to be him.

NURSE BAKER

You trust this man to depress your tongue? He gently cups your testicles and says cough?

WYATT

The face, the gestures, the voice. He can't be one of *them*. I refuse to believe it.

NURSE BAKER

I told you. They like to dress up, act out.

BUDGE

Act out what?

WYATT

I was with him when he bought those shoes. This is Dr. Bazelon. It has to be.

NURSE BAKER

A doctor of medicine? A private corporation? You're telling me this man is capable of winning a malpractice suit? He takes his beeper with him when he goes to the opera?

WYATT (*to Bazelon*)

Who are you? Tell me.

BUDGE

We depend on you people.

WYATT
We're hospital patients.

BUDGE
We're here to be reassured.

WYATT
We're at your mercy and you do this?

NURSE BAKER
Don't look at me.

WYATT
I'm looking at him.

Nurse Baker escorts Bazelon to the door.

NURSE BAKER
Gentlemen, time for lunch.

WYATT
Just when we think it's over, it begins again. If you're my doctor, give me a sign, say something, reveal yourself.

Dr. Bazelon is silent.

Nurse Baker opens the door.

They exit.

BUDGE
Let's put our heads together, shall we?

WYATT
I think I'm beyond conversation.

BUDGE

We have to discuss this, Mr. Wyatt. The only way to figure
this out is to work through the possibilities. Two of them as
I see it.

WYATT

What are they?

BUDGE

First. The man is from the Arno Klein Wing. A gifted
madman, let's say. A genius of mimicry and imitation.
Bazelon is affiliated with the hospital, am I right? He comes
here often, visits with his patients. The mimic has studied
him, perhaps for years. The mimic has followed him through
the corridors, perfecting the walk, the voice, the little
giveaway tics and trembles, the particularities. The man is
driven to impersonate. He suffers terribly. This is the crux of
his condition. Other people are his only grip on the world,
his only escape from fear. He is put away because his
impressions are so accurate, so shattering.

WYATT

You'll never get me to believe that wasn't Bazelon.

BUDGE

If you don't believe the first possibility, you'll never believe
the second.

WYATT

What is the second?

BUDGE

That was Bazelon.

WYATT

I don't believe it.

42

BUDGE

You've been saying all along it has to be him.

WYATT

True. But why would he behave that way, become mute, allow himself to be dragged out like that?

BUDGE

Let me attempt an explanation. Halting, groping—

WYATT

I know those shoes. I was with him when he bought those shoes.

BUDGE

Children sometimes develop a particular delusion. They imagine that everything that happens around them is taking place by prearrangement. Things exist only as they affect the child. The child imagines that when he turns a corner, everything behind him, everything he can no longer see and hear, simply collapses or vanishes or is folded up and carted away and stored somewhere. Buildings, automobiles, people. The next time he heads that way, word is relayed ahead, the streets and buildings reappear, reality is secured, at least for a time. Everything that exists is for the benefit, or the detriment, or the pleasure, or the horror, of the particular child.

WYATT

I used to imagine, listening to a ballgame, as a kid, on the radio, that when I turned the radio off, in the seventh inning, say, with two out, men on first and third, that everything sort of shut down at that point. It simply stopped.

BUDGE

We're moving right along. See? You're contributing.

WYATT

Then, when my father, or the person masquerading as my father, came home with the newspaper that evening, there was a resumption of the reality of the ballgame. I'd see a final score, a boxscore, printed in the paper, just for me, or so I'd imagine, with a detailed account of the game, complete with misprints, typographical errors, to make things totally, forever, convincing. Everything is managed for the child's consumption. His parents aren't really his parents.

BUDGE

His doctor isn't really his doctor.

WYATT

You're suggesting, in my case, the fantasy is true.

BUDGE

Your case is the only case.

WYATT

There was no ballgame, you're saying. Not even a ballpark. Just noises on the radio. Or *in* the radio. Dr. Bazelon was in his office only when I was scheduled for an appointment. The minute I left the office, they folded the whole thing up, put it in storage somewhere, on another level.

BUDGE

The set goes up, the set comes down.

WYATT

Then, today, somehow, you're saying, the system went awry.

BUDGE

Something happened. A warp of some kind. Or the structure collapsed too soon. I told you this was wildly implausible. It's easier to believe in the madman who impersonates.

44

WYATT

But he *is* Dr. Bazelon if he's anything.

BUDGE

But is he anything?

WYATT

And if I were to call home now, in this warp as you call it, what would happen? Would there be a wife and children there to answer? Nothing is beyond the telephone, you're saying. There's nothing out there. Some vastness I can't see or name.

BUDGE

I don't know anything you don't know.

WYATT

If everything has been set up, all my life, and if it's been running smoothly until today, when a defect suddenly appeared, then who are you, Mr. Budge, and what are you doing here?

BUDGE

All I'm doing is raising possibilities. Admittedly not very logical ones. But we're talking, we're interacting. I'm surprised and delighted by our progress.

WYATT

Progress toward what?

BUDGE

Undisguised talk. Transparency. The language of friends.

WYATT

I'm hungry.

BUDGE

Why don't you go into the corridor, see what's there?

WYATT

I'm only here for tests.

BUDGE

I'm a readmission.

WYATT

Bring us our food!

BUDGE

Why don't you ring the call bell? Ring the call bell.

WYATT

You ring the call bell. You go into the corridor.

BUDGE

What about the phone? Why don't you pick up the phone, just to listen?

WYATT

To find out if there's a dial tone, you mean.

BUDGE

What if there's nothing?

WYATT

There's always something. There's some kind of activity in there. Something an acoustical engineer can measure. If we can't hear it, an acoustical instrument can hear it. Or a dog. Or a bat. There has to be some kind of vibration.

BUDGE

What if there isn't?

WYATT

I checked myself in to be reassured.

46

BUDGE

The whole thing is problematical.

WYATT

I'm afraid.

BUDGE

So am I. We're both afraid. But we can talk, can't we? We can have a dialogue. In other words we're here, let's make the most of it. I remember an afternoon in Istanbul. I stood outside a café with tile murals. What dizzying conversation, what tumult of feeling. Dialogues so fervent I wanted to remove my shoes before entering. People gaze at each other. They practically melt together, saying the most familiar things. Every word fills a void. We only have to talk, Mr. Wyatt, to keep the world turning. The world at the tips of our fingers, the tip of our tongue. I sense a gradual willingness on your part. You're joining in nicely, developing an ease, a certain—

> *Nurse Baker enters with two orderlies wearing surgical masks. Although Wyatt's back is to the door and he can't see them, he gets up immediately and crosses his arms on his chest, as if straitjacketed.*
>
> *One of the orderlies approaches Wyatt and escorts him to the door. Nurse Baker and the other orderly quickly strip Wyatt's bed. They carry the blanket, sheets, mattress cover and pillow toward the door.*
>
> *All exit.*
>
> *Budge stands to watch them leave.*

No, no, no, no. Who are you? What is this? Don't leave. They're leaving. They've left.

He sits down.

I'm alone. Look at me. Abandoned.

> *Presently Mr. Grass enters, dragging with him the metal stand and bottles of intravenous solutions. Grass looks beyond the figure of Budge, as if toward some room off a second-story landing.*

GRASS

Darling, I'm home. The 5:55 was cancelled. I took the 6:66.

BUDGE

You look worse than ever.

GRASS

I've got Dutch elm disease. They want to treat it with fiber optics. Shoot me full of white light.

BUDGE

What amazes me is this. Your body is falling apart but your voice is strong.

GRASS

My voice isn't part of my body. It's what comes out of my body when I speak. It's the air which by some miracle we are able to shape into the sounds we wish to make.

BUDGE

A lovely insight. See? You're capable.

GRASS

Some people are genetically coded for greatness. Some are foreign-born. Some go to the racetrack every day, take the special train, study the form. What an interesting thing a horse is, when you think of it.

BUDGE

Who was the first person who decided to get on top of one?

GRASS

Exactly.

BUDGE

Scary.

GRASS

Right.

BUDGE

See? We're able to agree. People learn to adjust to each other. Civility is the keynote.

Grass looks into the middle distance.

GRASS

What's for dinner, sweetie? Did you pick up the dry cleaning? Why aren't the children here to greet me?

Budge goes to the telephone at the head of his bed.

BUDGE

I'm afraid.

GRASS

So am I. But why?

BUDGE

I'm calling home.

GRASS

Who's there?

BUDGE

No one's there. I'm dialing my number at home, just to see
if it rings.

GRASS

What if it doesn't ring?

BUDGE

That's what I'm afraid of.

GRASS

So am I.

Budge puts the receiver to his ear.

BUDGE

There's a dial tone. This is very encouraging.

GRASS

I'm encouraged.

BUDGE

I was afraid there would be nothing. Dead air. Soundless.

GRASS

There's hope.

BUDGE

There's noise.

*Budge dials the number. The phone on Wyatt's night
table rings. Budge is shocked, puts down the receiver.*

Grass mimics his fearful gesture.

GRASS

Don't look at me.

50

BUDGE

There's no one else to look at. Unless I go out there.

GRASS

You don't want to go out there.

BUDGE

What's out there?

GRASS

You don't want to know, you don't want to go.

BUDGE

What if I stick my head out the door?

GRASS

That counts as going. If you go out there, you may never come back. And if you go out again, you'll never come back again. And if you go out one more time, you'll never come back one more time. Take my advice.

Nurse Baker enters, slowly.

NURSE BAKER

We're taking you down now.

BUDGE

What?

GRASS

We're taking you down now.

> *Budge sits on the bed, wraps himself in sheets, both fists clenched against his mouth.*

NURSE BAKER

There's just so much time set aside for baffled reaction. I believe we've reached the limit.

BUDGE (*muffled*)

No, no, no, no.

NURSE BAKER

I understand what you're trying to say.

BUDGE

A hideous scream.

NURSE BAKER

Exactly.

BUDGE

A cry of desperation.

NURSE BAKER

Perfect.

BUDGE

A strangled sob. A plea torn from my throat. What sound can I make to convince you I'm not the one you want? A disconsolate sigh? Maybe that's what you want to hear. The smallest human moan imaginable. A whisper in a corner of an unlit room, with curtains blowing in the wind.

NURSE BAKER

What could be more touching?

GRASS

We're taking you down now.

NURSE BAKER

You want desperately to believe in appearances. You want the simplest assurances. I understand completely. So many cruel deceptions. Is there anyone you can believe in? Are you talking to the person you think you're talking to? Is the person saying what you think she's saying? In this case, my case, all it takes is a glance. What is the difference, Mr. Budge, between you and me? Is it sex, or color, or age? The deepest difference is the most superficial. I'm wearing a uniform, you are not. I have authority, you do not. In all the muddle of the world, in the mixed signals, the clash, the banter, the thinking of one thing and saying of another, the saying of one thing and meaning of another, in all these lies and poems and civilizations, in all this razzle—it's the uniform that matters. The person in the uniform controls the facts. That's what uniforms are for. They prove that truth is possible. People who wear the same uniforms know the same things. People who wear different uniforms know different things and you can tell who knows what by the uniforms they wear. White means one thing, blue means another. You can see my authority with the naked eye. Look, right here, unmistakable, intact. (*Waits*) There's just so much time set aside for helpful explanations.

GRASS

I believe we've reached the limit.

NURSE BAKER

We're taking you down now.

The two masked orderlies enter, slip in behind Nurse Baker, seize her arms. She struggles briefly, then goes limp.

The orderlies drag her out.

GRASS

We sold our apartment the day after we bought it. Made a brilliant killing. I'm trying to buy the air rights over Lake Michigan. A metaphysical coup. There is real estate and unreal estate.

BUDGE

All right. I'll take your advice.

GRASS

Take my advice. If you go out there ten times, you'll never come back once for each time you go out. This is called set theory.

Budge sits in one of the chairs.

BUDGE

Although I'm not sure I should listen. How can I trust you?

GRASS

How can I trust myself?

BUDGE

Who's in control?

GRASS

That's what I fail to ask myself every hour on the half hour.

BUDGE

You're part of the whole thing.

GRASS

Whatever the whole thing is.

BUDGE

Exactly.

GRASS

Scary.

BUDGE

Right.

GRASS

The children don't greet me at the door, now that they're grown. They grow so fast. My daughter is almost as old as I am. Smart as a whip. She thinks I'm unreasonable. She can't greet me at the door, she says, now that she's middle-aged, with children of her own. She has a station wagon. Why can't she drive down in her station wagon, from the hill country, for two measly minutes, to stand—

BUDGE

At the door.

GRASS

—when I come home, with my recycled fluids, after a day at the office? Her own children are grown. They have children of their own. Her children's children still greet her children when *they* come home from the office, at the door. Some people study the form. They follow the horses south.

BUDGE

See? We're making headway.

GRASS

I'll need a bed.

BUDGE

You can use Mr. Wyatt's bed. It's an excellent bed, for what it is.

GRASS

What is it?

BUDGE

I have two sheets. I'll give you one. I'm happy to share.

GRASS

I don't have a blanket.

BUDGE

I'll give you my blanket. I don't need a blanket.

GRASS

Will you give me your pillow?

BUDGE

I don't use a pillow. I sleep without a pillow. See? It's perfect. It works out beautifully.

GRASS

Will you tell me a story before I go to sleep?

BUDGE

Ha ha ha ha ha ha ha.

GRASS

Ha ha ha ha ha ha ha.

BUDGE

Come. Sit down. We'll talk.

Grass slowly makes his way toward a chair.

Black.

ACT TWO

Figure in straitjacket

Desk clerk

Maid

Gary, a young man

Lynette, a young woman

Freddie, a man of indeterminate age

Manville, a man in his forties

Jolene, a black woman

Arno Klein, a man in his sixties

NOTE: In the motel sequence, an actor in a straitjacket functions as the TV set. He is the same actor who is cast as Wyatt in Act One.

Evening.

A large white space flooded in harsh fluorescent light.
White furniture is arranged in a pile, chaotically.
There is a stepladder. Crayons and drawing paper are
scattered on the floor. Streaks of food and other
suspicious matter cover the back wall. There is a door
at either end of the wall.

This is the day room in the Arno Klein Wing.

A man in a straitjacket sits in a wheeled swivel chair.
His hair is closely cropped and he is extremely pale.
He stares straight ahead, motionless.

*A woman enters from the wings, pushing a
supermarket cart. A man sits in the cart, carrying a
large broom. They wear old clothes. She dips the
cart to let him out.*

*The man sweeps crayons and other debris into the
wings. The woman begins to remove furniture from
the pile.*

DESK CLERK
Because I won't be here. Now that you bring it up.

MAID
Where will you be?

DESK CLERK

I'm going to California to help a friend commit suicide.

They begin to arrange the furniture.

MAID

I mean my God. It can't be that simple.

DESK CLERK

I didn't say it was simple. It could be a tremendous mess. Like stuff is gurgling out of his throat. We'll just have to see.

MAID

But the way you say it. I'm concerned by that.

DESK CLERK

How do you want me to say it?

MAID

I don't know.

DESK CLERK

How do you say something like that?

MAID

I don't know. Build up to it.

DESK CLERK

How would you say it?

MAID

I mean my God. Is it male or female at least?

DESK CLERK

It's a buddy. A friend of mine I used to know.

*They position two beds, several chairs, a lamp and a
night table in a compact area center stage.*

MAID

You just get on a plane? I'm trying to picture this. How do
you pack for a suicide?

DESK CLERK

Look, I didn't volunteer. He asked me do I want to do it. It
was his idea. He *sent* me a ticket. It's something he feels he
has to experience.

MAID

Well, I can't decide if this is horrible or what.

DESK CLERK

Be sure to let me know.

MAID

All right. How does he want to do it?

DESK CLERK

We have to have a meeting of the minds. I've got some
interesting ideas.

*They hang a section of venetian blinds in front of the
back wall.*

MAID

Do we have names in this?

DESK CLERK

No.

MAID

What are we?

DESK CLERK
I'm the desk clerk, you're the maid.

The man opens the drawer of a night table, takes out a telephone, places it on the table.

MAID
Why does he need help to do it? Why can't he do it alone? Maybe he wants you to talk him out of it. Talk him out of it.

DESK CLERK
How do I talk him out of it?

MAID
I don't know. Speak softly. Wear cheerful colors.

The woman strips white fabric from the beds, revealing garish coverlets beneath.

I guess I'm supposed to ask why he wants to do it in the first place, so I can show a little empathy. I'd like to believe he has a solid reason. There's a childhood scar. There's a nightmare illness. His marriage is crashing down. His career is flattening out. He doesn't feel good about his total package. But that doesn't explain why he needs a buddy. Is he a Vietnam vet? It sounds like Vietnam.

DESK CLERK
He's an actor, as a matter of fact. Not that I didn't tell him from the start. Acting is dangerous.

We see a smallish motel room.

The man adjusts the position of the straitjacketed figure, which is the room TV. Then he takes a remote control device out of his pocket and leaves it on a table near the TV set.

The woman folds the stepladder, picks it up and exits through the wings.

The man touches a dimmer on the wall. The lights come way down. He exits, pushing the supermarket cart.

Silence.

Gary enters through a door. He carries an overnight bag, which he deposits on one of the beds. He tosses a room key on the other bed and switches on a lamp. Automatically he picks up the remote control device and aims it at the TV set, turning the set on. Without waiting to see or hear what comes on, he goes into the bathroom, using the door opposite the entrance.

TV

Now purse your lips. I want you to purse your lips. That's right. Now say ooooh.

Ooooh.

Now stretch. I want you to stretch wide. Eeeee. Let me hear it.

Eeeee.

Once more.

Eeeee.

That's good. That's very good.

Eeeee.

Now open wide. Give me a nice big aaaah.

Aaaah.

Come on.

Aaaah.

Lynette enters, a little bedraggled, in beat-up clothes, and carrying a shoulder bag, handbag and jacket. She puts things down, sits in a chair, gazes at the TV.

That's very nice. That's super.

Aaaah.

We're coming along. We're doing very nicely.

Aaaah.

You're responding wonderfully. You're a therapist's dream.

Aaaah.

Lips together now. Lips touching. Now sort of pop them open softly. Baaaa. Come on. You can do it. Softly.

Baaaa.

Once again, please.

Baaaa.

We're learning to talk all over again. It's not so very hard, is it? Baaaa.

Baaaa.

Aaaah.

Aaaah.

Gary comes out, drying his face with a towel. Lynette turns off the set.

GARY
I was thinking the other day. Funny. You never see an old man named Gary.

LYNETTE
The trouble is I can't fall asleep in a strange bed the first night, no matter how tired I am.

GARY

It's not an old man's name. We don't last that long. But that's not the problem.

LYNETTE

It's like I hear a buzz coming from the sheets.

GARY

I like strange beds. The problem is I don't want to be here.

LYNETTE

I am enormously hungry.

GARY

I walked in the door and thought what for.

LYNETTE

Well, I'm looking forward to this. And I'm going to be darkly disappointed if they're not here.

GARY

Manville sounded pretty certain.

LYNETTE

I'm going to be a broken woman. After so many tries. Because they're very, very elusive.

GARY

That's the point.

LYNETTE

People who've actually seen them are about as hard to find as they are. I don't know anyone who's seen them.

GARY

That's the appeal, Lynette.

LYNETTE

Shouldn't there be a friend of a friend somewhere who's reportedly seen them? Even if he's mistaken or lying. Even the most unreliable word.

GARY

Manville wouldn't have called if he wasn't sure.

LYNETTE

But he hasn't actually seen them.

GARY

He knows they're here. He says they're here. He's relatively certain.

LYNETTE

When I was in Amsterdam I heard they were in London. You know me. Run right to the airport. Get to London, not a trace. I called all over town. Scoured the city in taxis like a raving whatever. The drivers seemed to understand. They seemed to *like* the idea. But all they could do was drive me through back streets, back alleys, the only obvious places to look.

GARY

You never see a kid with a grandfather named Gary.

LYNETTE

Taxi after taxi. Not one single driver had even *heard* of the group.

GARY

Nobody says they're great theater.

LYNETTE

We asked people on the street. I called up to windows.

66

GARY

People say, "Elusive, mysterious, unsettling."

LYNETTE

It's unsettling because you can't find them. This is what
makes it unsettling.

GARY

It was dumb not to stop for dinner.

LYNETTE

We can get something to eat once we find out where they
are. But I know I won't sleep.

GARY

Sheets of rain.

LYNETTE

What did Manville say exactly, word for word?

GARY

Only that they're here.

LYNETTE

I've been trying to see this group for half my life, it seems.

GARY

Who do you know in London?

LYNETTE

We all know someone in London.

GARY

You said you called all over town.

LYNETTE

Just an expression, love.

Now that we're finally here, I'm thinking so what.

He picks up the device, turns on the TV.

TV

It affects my husband. It affects our relationship. It affects our children. It affects our friends. It affects the people I work with. It affects—

He aims the device, changes channels.

—in a setting remarkably like that of Shakespeare's day.

Click.

One question I'm always asked: Jane, what do I wear to a second wedding?

Click.

France needs you. I need you.

Click.

It was many months before the gorillas began to accept her.

Click.

Bong. Bong. Bong. Canterbury cathedral. Nearly destroyed by Henry VIII and again by the bomber squadrons of the Luftwaffe in World War II. Bong. Bong.

He turns it off.

LYNETTE

We drive three hundred miles to see a play put on by a

company nobody can ever find. You want to watch
television.

GARY

I never watch television. I listen to it. The whole point of
TV is the audio.

LYNETTE

I am fabulously hungry.

GARY

Maybe I can find a take-out place.

LYNETTE

I don't want to eat. I want to talk about it.

GARY

The idea is interesting. I'll say that.

LYNETTE

I missed them in London. I may have missed them in Cairo,
although I don't think they ever showed up. When I was in
Santa Fe staying with my sister, I kept hearing rumors they
were in town.

GARY

They're following you.

LYNETTE

I'm right here.

GARY

The idea has merit. They're out there, doing whatever they
do, whether we show up or not. When were you in Cairo?

LYNETTE

It was the London trip. I went to Cairo. There was a man
in the desert sweeping sand.

GARY

I didn't know you had a sister.

LYNETTE

She's the sisterly one. I'm the one you take to motels.
Shouldn't we be making phone calls?

GARY

Manville will know where they are.

LYNETTE

You have confidence in this fellow.

GARY

He'll meet us here, take us to the theater, buy us a drink
somewhere.

LYNETTE

Is there a theater in a town like this? Do they perform in
theaters? I have a feeling that's the last place to look for
them.

GARY

I'm satisfied just imagining they exist.

A knock on the door.

Perfect timing.

Gary opens the door.

*Freddie enters, wearing a shabby dark suit, dark
sneakers, thick eyeglasses—wild-haired, intense,
rabbinical.*

Who are you?

FREDDIE

Just Freddie, I guess, for now.

GARY

Where's Manville?

FREDDIE

We have to pick him up. Don't worry. It's all worked out.

GARY

He never told me about a Freddie.

FREDDIE

I've known Manville many years.

GARY

I've known Manville many years.

FREDDIE

I said it first.

LYNETTE

Does he know where the Arno Klein group is? We're here to
see a play.

GARY

Eight hours on the turnpike.

LYNETTE

Miles of road repair.

GARY

Lashing rain.

FREDDIE

I'm not surprised. There are people who track this company
in a serious way.

LYNETTE

I'm relieved to hear I'm not the only one.

GARY

I'm interested in the mystery of the thing. That's enough for me.

LYNETTE

Not me, pal. I want to be there. I want the experience. The experience is supposed to be so powerful. I looked for them in Cairo. I was told to find a café with a dirt floor. I took a taxi to the edge of the desert. The driver had postcards of New York taped and pasted everywhere. An old man with a broom was fifty yards up ahead, sweeping sand off the road. This is an actual job they do with brooms on a regular basis—keep the desert out. The driver offered me a fig.

FREDDIE

Did you ever think that might be *them?* The taxi man and sweeper. That was possibly the spot.

LYNETTE

I am so bloody hungry.

FREDDIE

Because they are not necessarily easy to identify.

LYNETTE

That's for sure.

GARY

That's the point.

LYNETTE

Whenever I think I've forgotten the whole thing, someone calls and tells me they're in such and such a city, or I see their name in a newspaper, the tiniest mention. The tiniest mention sets me off.

GARY

Obsessed women are fun to watch.

                    LYNETTE
Maybe they're just a never-ending rumor.

                    FREDDIE
They're not.

                    GARY
We've never met anyone who's seen them.

                    LYNETTE
No one I know has ever been able to tell me, absolutely,
once and for all, that there is such a thing as the Arno Klein
Theater.

                    FREDDIE
There is.

                    GARY
How do you know?

                    FREDDIE
I've seen them.

                    LYNETTE
Where?

                    FREDDIE
I saw the London performance.

                    LYNETTE
When?

                    FREDDIE
Three years ago.

                    LYNETTE
But that's when I was there. I searched alleys and

73

warehouses. I called up to second-story windows. People were wonderful about it.

FREDDIE
I'll tell you what your mistake was.

LYNETTE
What?

FREDDIE
The London performance took place in Amsterdam. People flew to Amsterdam.

LYNETTE
I was in Amsterdam. I flew to London.

FREDDIE
That was your mistake. You were supposed to fly to Amsterdam. Search back streets, back canals.

LYNETTE
I'm a totally broken woman.

FREDDIE
This is what they do. They turn up in some remote part of the city. They simply appear. In Amsterdam they used squatters' buildings. A different building every night. A different back canal.

LYNETTE
What was it like?

FREDDIE
It changed my life. Can't you tell?

GARY
The idea is nice. I like the idea.

74

LYNETTE
Taxi after taxi.

FREDDIE
Before Amsterdam I was an ordinary man. I spoke to people
in a normal tongue. I did the ordinary things. Sunsets, lunch,
escalators. I fed the neighbor's cat when the neighbor was
away. There's none of that now. I took a bath every day,
naked, a man with a history, ordinary Fred. That seems so
faraway. There were edges and separations. I borrowed books
and took the train to Middletown. A spoon was not a
painting of a spoon. All that is lost to me now.

LYNETTE
What is left?

FREDDIE
I talk to imaginary men, to ghosts on battlements. I accept
it all. I believe it all. Dreams, facts, accidents, dizzy spells,
paranoid fantasies, mirages in the desert. A mirage is water
and the illusion of water. God isn't some rumor drifting
down the street. God happens all the time. There are large
and small gods. Multicolored gods. They eat breakfast, they
live in the sky, they take monkey form and human form.
Everything is true. Everything can and does and will
happen, maybe a million times a second. Look at me. True
or false?

LYNETTE
True.

FREDDIE
I've reduced everything to this.

GARY
To what?

FREDDIE

This body. That room.

LYNETTE

What room?

FREDDIE

Just along the hall.

GARY

You have a room here?

FREDDIE

I live here.

GARY

In the motel.

FREDDIE

If that's what we've agreed to call it.

LYNETTE

But it must be depressing.

GARY

Everything's standardized.

LYNETTE

Nothing's really yours.

FREDDIE

One place is as good as another. How different can two places be if we use the word "place" in both cases? We can change places without changing words. We don't even have to change places. We don't have to move from the room.

GARY

I'm convinced we'll never find them. They don't want to be found. There's something pure in that.

LYNETTE

Pure crap.

GARY

It has an open-endedness.

LYNETTE

I know I won't sleep.

GARY

Actors, but who?

LYNETTE

Meanwhile.

GARY

Where's Manville?

FREDDIE

It's still early.

LYNETTE

I'd like to clean up and rest awhile. Tell you what. Find Manville, come back for me, we'll set out together. All right, Freddie?

FREDDIE

Half an hour.

LYNETTE

Half an hour.

GARY

We should have eaten on the road.

Gary and Freddie exit.

*Lynette picks up the remote control device and turns
on the TV, sitting extremely close to the set.*

TV

—except in the case of a major frontal impact, where the
driver's head rockets toward the windshield at a speed
exceeding—

Click.

Promiscuous grandparents, for example.

Click.

The robot's arm speaks a kind of arm language. This is the
only language—

Click.

There's no reason why grocery shopping can't be a shared
experience. The average day is filled with opportunities for
sharing. The American home can be a sharing place. Make a
checklist of things you can share and keep it in a highly
visible spot. A magnetic memo clipboard attached to your
refrigerator or other major appliance is a good place to keep
your list of shared activities. Update your list periodically.
Read aloud from your list. Invent games and contests based
on your list. Think about extending your list—

Click.

But Mao rejected Lenin's model of revolution.

Click.

This is the only language the arm understands. If we want to move the robot's leg, we enter a completely different subroutine.

Click.

It affects me. It affects my husband. It affects—

Click.

Nytex, Westlab, Telcon, Syntech, Microdyne.

Click.

We're talking pound after pound after pound.

Click.

Lackluster industrials.

Click.

Irreversible comas.

Click.

Saturated fats.

Click.

But Betty never suspected that the bottle with the blue detergent—

Click.

Now hold the paper and get ready to make your *h*. Put
your pencil on the baseline and make your *h* to the
numerical count of seven. Here we go. Undercurve, loop,
slant, pause, retrace, overcurve, slant. Look at your *h*. Look
at my *h*. We can use the letter *h* in the word "horse." Here
is the word "horse." You all know what a horse looks like.
This is what the word looks like. Is there anyone who sees
a resemblance?

> *A knock on the door. Lynette turns off the TV.*
> *Manville enters, wearing a designer warmup suit.*

LYNETTE

Where's Gary?

MANVILLE

I sent him on a mission with Freddie. To locate a contact of
mine. A key figure in this whole affair.

LYNETTE

Does anyone know what time this play gets started?

MANVILLE

Is there a starting time?

LYNETTE

I don't know. Is there? Or does it just happen?

MANVILLE

I'm saying to myself so this is Gary's lady friend. So she and
Gary. I've often wondered. I've tried to picture the woman
he would finally allow me to see. I thought to myself so
Gary's entered a situation. He's taking a look at the serious
side.

LYNETTE

We met in a museum. He goes to museums to meet women.

80

MANVILLE
Learned it from me. A museum. A rainy day.

LYNETTE
Men follow me through museums. They think I won't mind,
surrounded by serious art.

MANVILLE
Our dirty thoughts are concealed in the high-minded air.

LYNETTE
I'm supposed to believe if a man is in a museum, he is
wonderfully sensitive and intelligent. We have sensitive
things to say to each other. An afternoon of intelligent sex is
sure to follow. It's just a question of finding a taxi.

MANVILLE
On a rainy day. What happened?

LYNETTE
We barely knew each other.

MANVILLE
I love to talk to women I barely know. They're practically
the only people I talk to. I love to hear a woman say,
"Theater is my life." I believe remarks like that.

LYNETTE
But theater is not my life.

MANVILLE
You got on a plane. Flew to London to see a play.

LYNETTE
What better reason for rash acts?

MANVILLE
Tell me about yourself. Make it up. Who are you? What do

you want? What are your hopes, dreams, fears, ambitions?
Use clichés. Tell me something I can believe.

LYNETTE

Is this how you seduce a woman? Play to her self-absorption.

MANVILLE

Some women.

LYNETTE

Others respond differently. They don't think museums on
rainy days are terribly sexy.

MANVILLE

Tell me what's sexy.

LYNETTE

Motels.

MANVILLE

We're moving right along.

LYNETTE

It's a night spent precisely nowhere.

MANVILLE

Do you know what I'm saying to myself? Sensibility. Nuance
and texture. A long, subtle, textured conversation, with a
woman of sensibility, in a cheap motel.

LYNETTE

And I absolutely have to see this company?

MANVILLE

Oh God yes.

LYNETTE

I've never been this close.

MANVILLE

You're closer than you think.

LYNETTE

What do you mean?

MANVILLE

I happen to know a member of the troupe. She'll tell us
exactly where the play is being done.

LYNETTE

Fantastic.

Manville rummages through Gary's bag.

MANVILLE

This is their deepest secret. People travel great distances.
Passionate about theater. Drawn by a rumor, a whisper. They
finally arrive. No sign of Arno Klein. People go a little
wacky. "We know they're close. We feel it. The air is
charged. But where are they?"

LYNETTE

Where are they?

MANVILLE

It could be a barricaded room, a train depot abandoned for
years. Tonight we find out. Jolene is a brilliant actress and
old friend. Freddie's making contact right now. He'll bring
her here. She'll lead us right to the spot.

Manville pulls a couple of shirts out of Gary's bag.
Some toiletries, some magazines, a hair-dryer. He takes

*a magazine to the chair by the door, begins to turn
pages.*

LYNETTE

I used to be a frosted blond. You know why? I liked the
sound of it.

MANVILLE

Do this for me. Say, "My skin is alabaster." Describe your
body for me. Believable language. That's what we want.

LYNETTE

My skin is alabaster.

MANVILLE

My breasts.

LYNETTE

My breasts are large and ripe. Straining against the tight
dress. Tumbling free.

MANVILLE

Buttocks.

LYNETTE

My buttocks are small, clenched, firm.

MANVILLE

Legs.

LYNETTE

I have long legs. My thighs are smooth and supple. My hips
rounded, supple, smooth.

MANVILLE

Say, "Creamy white."

LYNETTE

My belly is creamy white. The whitest part of me.

MANVILLE

Say, "Velvety smooth."

LYNETTE

My thighs are supple. Velvety smooth. I have long legs. My skin is alabaster.

MANVILLE

Recite to me.

LYNETTE

My lips are wet, sensual, shiny bright.

MANVILLE

My nipples.

LYNETTE

My nipples are firm, tilted. My hips rounded, supple, smooth. I have frosted blond hair that spills over my shoulders. My eyes are dark. The darkest part of me.

MANVILLE

I rake my nails.

LYNETTE

I rake my nails across his broad back.

MANVILLE

Breasts. Breasts.

LYNETTE

My belly is creamy white. My breasts strain against the tight red dress. They tumble free. Rounded, supple, smooth.

MANVILLE
Make me feel secure.

LYNETTE
My dress is slit to the thigh. I have long legs. My skin is alabaster. My eyes are dark and wild and smoky.

MANVILLE
Night creature's eyes.

LYNETTE
I rake my nails across his broad back. I cry out. My mouth is bright and wet.

MANVILLE
Language we can trust.

LYNETTE
My voice is breathless with excitement.

They sit motionless, not looking at each other.

Gary enters, carrying take-out food in a paper bag. He studies the scene carefully.

Lynette turns on the TV.

TV
I'm getting mixed messages about my sexuality.

She turns it off.

MANVILLE
Meanwhile.

LYNETTE
Where's Freddie?

GARY

Still looking.

LYNETTE

Why are these people so damn hard to find?

GARY

Maybe they just resist consumption.

MANVILLE

Maybe they can't find a decent place.

GARY

They're poor, they're strange, they're afraid.

LYNETTE

We drove all day.

GARY

Sheets of rain.

LYNETTE

Oil drums painted orange.

GARY

It's running through my head. Caution caution caution.
Toll booth three hundred yards. Narrow bridge. Sweet
corn. School crossing.

LYNETTE

Heavy rain.

GARY

I don't want to find them. I want to imagine them,
dream them, hear their name in a crowd.

A knock on the door.

No one moves to open it.

Jolene walks in, shaking out an umbrella, flamboyantly dressed and made-up.

JOLENE
You people are awful hard to find. I've been looking all over.

MANVILLE
Jolene, hello. What a surprise.

LYNETTE
Well, are we glad to see you. Talk to us. We want to know everything. Tell us what to expect.

Gary hands out food.

JOLENE
Nothing happens till Klein shows up.

LYNETTE
Is there a person? I thought it was just a name.

JOLENE
There's a Klein all right. Everything we do is Klein. We only do one play. We do it over and over. It's the only thing we know.

LYNETTE
Is he a working member? Does he act?

JOLENE
Does he ever stop acting?

LYNETTE
Well, where is he?

JOLENE

Don't worry. He'll show up. He likes to be late.

LYNETTE

What about the other actors?

JOLENE

You don't want to know about actors. Actors are depressing.
We're unhappy people. We lead terrible lives. What is that?

GARY

Boiled dumplings.

MANVILLE

Better eat, Jolene. You can't get a meal after a certain hour
in a town like this.

LYNETTE

What terrible lives? I admire actors.

JOLENE

Don't get me started on the subject of actors.

LYNETTE

Are you telling me you'd rather do something else?

JOLENE

It's a subject I hate.

LYNETTE

What would you rather do?

JOLENE

It's a desperate life.

LYNETTE

But the words alone. The speeches.

JOLENE

I hate speeches. Look. Let me put it this way. When an
athlete dies young, it's a terrible twist of nature. Something
incoherent trails the event. You're left a little stunned. This
boy or girl is a demon runner. Let her run. Let him jump his
hurdles. It's all so innocent and swift. How different for an
actor. Young, old, ancient, budding, decrepit. Dying is what
we're all about. Remember the first body you ever saw, laid
out, when you were little? All made-up. Rouged and waxed
and clown-white. The last little slick of concealment. Well,
here we are, sweetheart. We show you how to hide from
what you know. There's no innocence here. Just secrets,
terrors, deceptions. That's all I have to say. I've said too
much. It's too damn grim.

She takes a bite of food.

Look. We're just like everybody else, only quicker to pick up
a danger. That's what makes an actor in the first place. That
little rap of panic in the chest. We develop techniques to
shield us from the facts. But they become the facts. The fear
is so deep we find it waiting in the smallest role. We can't
meet death on our own terms. We have no terms. Our
speeches rattle in our throats. We're robbed of all
consolations. Our only hope is other people. A handful, a
scatter, sitting here and there, day or night—still, gray,
nameless, waiting. But the parts we play in order to live
make us tremble in our own skin. We're transparent. This is
our mystery, our beauty, our genius, our sickness. According
to Klein.

She licks her finger.

We go on tonight, an hour from now, in a hospital right
here in town. The psychiatric wing. There's a room called
the day room. They don't use it at night. We've arranged to
borrow it, transform it, do our play, disappear. Now you
know.

90

She moves to the door.

Freddie is standing there.

MANVILLE

Thanks so much, Jolene. I promised these people. I said to
Gary on the phone—

GARY

He guaranteed it. I told Lynette.

LYNETTE

He said Manville sounded certain.

JOLENE

In an hour.

MANVILLE

In an hour.

Jolene exits.

Freddie walks in.

FREDDIE

Don't you know who that was? Didn't anybody recognize?

MANVILLE

What do you mean?

GARY

Who was it?

FREDDIE

Is it possible she sat right here? She talked to us, she ate our
food? And nobody knows who it was?

GARY

Who was it?

FREDDIE

The nurse. From the other wing.

MANVILLE

The other wing?

LYNETTE

What nurse?

GARY

What other wing?

FREDDIE

The black nurse. Pretending she's us.

GARY

What black nurse?

FREDDIE

In the white uniform.

LYNETTE

She wasn't wearing a uniform.

GARY

She was dressed like us.

LYNETTE

We're all dressed like us.

MANVILLE

We are us.

FREDDIE (to TV)

Have I remembered something we were all supposed to forget? Don't they know there's more than one wing. There's another and another and another and another.

Insanity's so personal. It's hard to know who shares our
secrets.

GARY

I want the mystery to linger.

FREDDIE

But I've seen them, remember, Amsterdam.

LYNETTE

We don't want to hear.

FREDDIE

I can ruin it for you just like that.

MANVILLE

Shut up, Freddie.

FREDDIE

I know their little tricks and trickettes.

GARY

I want them to escape.

FREDDIE

I can stop things cold with a well-constructed sentence.

MANVILLE

They drove all day.

LYNETTE

I'm counting on this night.

FREDDIE

I can shut this whole thing down right now.

Gary slings food at Freddie.

MANVILLE
Hey hey hey hey.

> *Freddie takes one step back, fastidiously hurls food at Gary.*

LYNETTE
I don't see the point.

MANVILLE
That's it. Come on. Enough.

> *Freddie steps back, throws plastic utensils at Gary's feet. Gary hurls his sandwich.*

> *The desk clerk appears in the doorway, unnoticed.*

GARY
This is making me self-conscious.

LYNETTE
I'm not watching, so just stop.

MANVILLE
Come on. Be smart. That's it.

> *Gary snatches food off the floor and throws it at Freddie, who covers up.*

FREDDIE
Can't you see I'm not athletic?

LYNETTE
I'm not interested in this.

MANVILLE
It's over. Enough. Come on.

Manville shields Freddie, holds on to him.

Lynette notices the desk clerk.

LYNETTE
Who are you?

DESK CLERK
The night man. Downstairs. At the desk.

MANVILLE
He looks like the night man. He looks like the
three-o'clock-in-the-morning man.

LYNETTE *(to Gary)*
Let's see the play, then head straight home. We'll drive
right through. I don't want to spend the night here anyway.

DESK CLERK
Good. We need the room.

GARY
Good. You can have it.

Lynette and Gary begin to gather their things.

DESK CLERK
Did you use the beds?

GARY
Does it look like we used the beds?

DESK CLERK
Well, I don't know. Some people are more cunning than
others. We get all kinds of stains, you know. After a while,
you learn how to tell one from another. Every emission and
secretion of the body ends up on motel sheets, sooner or

later. No matter how many times you wash the sheets, you can still see the outlines of certain stains. Some secretions don't ever wash out. You can beat the sheets on rocks. You can steam them in vats. Look real close next time you're in a motel bed. There's always an outline or two, shaped like islands in the sun. People come in, they pay their money, they make their stains and they go back home. That's what we're here for. This whole building was built so you would have a place to deposit your stains in secret.

                    LYNETTE
I think I'm ready.

                    GARY
Lead the way, Manville.

                    MANVILLE
Come on, Freddie.

        All four exit with their belongings.

        *The desk clerk sits in front of the TV set, staring
        intently at the screen face.*

        He turns on the set.

                    TV
It affects our children. It affects our friends. It affects the people I work with.

        Click.

First, keep your dissecting tools in a plastic baggie. Second, get to know your frog. Third—

        Click.

Little angry people grow up to be what? Big angry people.
Angry adults. Angry men and angry women.

Click.

Foam enhancers, stabilizers, conditioners, preservatives.

Click.

I think what Jessica is basically saying is that no matter how
brief the relationship is, you would want to know something
about your partner so you can experience your sexuality
without guilt or fear, anxiety or remorse, depression or worry,
dread or woe.

Click.

It affects me. It affects—

> *The maid enters, in uniform, wheeling a laundry cart.
> The desk clerk turns off the TV.*
>
> *The maid removes the dark bedspreads, revealing
> another set of coverlets beneath—lighter in color.*

MAID
It got dark so fast.

DESK CLERK
We call this "night."

> *She throws the dark fabric into the laundry cart.*

MAID
Where's Klein?

DESK CLERK

He'll be here.

The desk clerk cleans up the food mess on the floor.

The maid opens a night-table drawer and takes out a second room phone.

Want to see something weird?

MAID

Okay.

The desk clerk points to a chair.

DESK CLERK

What's that?

MAID

A chair.

He kicks the chair.

DESK CLERK

If it's a chair, why did I kick it?

Long pause.

MAID

It must be something else.

Long pause.

DESK CLERK

Exactly.

MAID

Scary.

DESK CLERK

Right.

> *Arno Klein enters. He and the desk clerk exchange a look of recognition.*
>
> *Klein carries an old-fashioned traveling bag. He wears a mustache, somewhat bohemian garb—long coat, slouch hat, scarf.*
>
> *He opens the suitcase, removes a smaller bag, deposits the suitcase under a bed. Then he turns on the TV, takes the smaller bag into the bathroom.*
>
> *The desk clerk and the maid continue their work in deep shadow.*
>
> *The TV sits in bright light.*

TV

But you *can* view the eclipse safely. There are three ways to do this. The first and simplest way is to take two squares of white cardboard, make a pinhole in one square.

Stretch wide now. Stretch wide. Eeeee.

(*Weakly*) Eeeee.

Can't hear you.

(*Weakly*) Eeeee.

One more time please. Come on now. Do it for me. You can do it.

Based on actual events in the life.

It affects my husband. It affects our relationship. It affects our children. It affects our friends.

I have nothing left to give, Richard.

Finally, you can make a pinhole box camera. First you obtain a grocery carton. Then you fasten a sheet of white paper to the inside of the carton, as you see here. Cut a one-inch hole near the top of the opposite end and cover it with aluminum foil. Make a pinhole in the foil. Seal the area around the pinhole with black tape, to keep out unwanted light. Cut a hole in the bottom of the box large enough to slip the box over your head. Slip the box over your head, keeping it tilted so that the concentrated ray of light does not burn a smoky hole in the back of your head. Then stand with your back to the sun and watch the image projected on the white sheet. Some people like to keep the box on their head even after the eclipse is over. Some people never remove the box. Some people live out their days with the box on their head, waiting for another eclipse, or just looking at the sheet of white paper on the inside of the box. Some people say the sheet of white paper is more interesting and educational when there is no eclipse taking place. They remove the box only for eclipses. They look directly into the sun. Remember, the sun is not the same as a paper cutout of the sun. Some people know this intuitively. Some go to night school. Some play checkers on stone tables in the park.

Repeat after me. Eeeee. Come on. Do it for me. Eeeee. Please do it. I know you can do it. I'm right here. I'm ready. If you really try, you can do it. Try hard. Please try. I'm listening. I'm waiting.

Silence.

Lights slowly up.

The desk clerk and maid are gone.

We see the hospital room of Act One.

Arno Klein emerges from the bathroom in slippers and

white pajamas, as Budge. He carries the small bag, slips it under a bed.

The straitjacketed figure is lost in shadow.

Budge begins to do a round of exercises, the ancient Chinese discipline known as tai chi.

His motions are slow, stylized, continuous, with a weightless quality. He does movements called "Draw the Bow" and "Wave Hands Like Clouds."

Black.